David's Crown

Also by Malcolm Guite

David's Crown

Sounding the Psalms

Malcolm Guite

CANTERBURY
PRESS
Norwich

© Malcolm Guite 2021

First published in 2021 by the Canterbury Press Norwich
Editorial office
3rd Floor, Invicta House
108–114 Golden Lane
London EC1Y 0TG, UK
www.canterburypress.co.uk

Canterbury Press is an imprint of Hymns Ancient & Modern Ltd
(a registered charity)

Hymns Ancient & Modern® is a registered trademark of
Hymns Ancient & Modern Ltd
13A Hellesdon Park Road, Norwich,
Norfolk NR6 5DR, UK

British Library Cataloguing in Publication data

A catalogue record for this book is available
from the British Library

978 1 78622 306 7

Typeset by Regent Typesetting
Printed and bound in Great Britain by
CPI Group (UK) Ltd

Contents

Deign at my hands this crown of prayer and praise.
John Donne, *La Corona*

Lift up my soul, and breathe through my poor rhymes
That I might lay these lines before your throne,
A frail corona wreathed of fading flowers
To set against the gold of David's crown.
LXXXVI *Inclina, Domine*

Preface

Like many people, I have found that the experience of crisis and darkness of living through the corona virus pandemic has brought my reading of Scripture to life and especially my engagement with the Psalter. Familiar words, recited by rote, have suddenly taken on power and resonance: pleas for help and mercy, confessions of despair, longings for renewal, thanksgivings for recovery, heart-felt cries for justice; all these passages in psalms which we may have recited almost absent-mindedly in happier years have become once more what they were always intended to be – the direct speech of the heart. And in this we are not making a new discovery but returning to a great tradition.

The psalms form part of our cycle of daily prayer in the Church of England, but that practice is only a late flowering of a much longer tradition. The regular recitation of the psalms reaches back deep into Judaism, forms part of the spiritual life of Christ himself, and was a staple of Christian worship from the earliest times, especially in the emergence of monastic communities, almost all of which make the recitation of the entire psalter the very centre of the turning wheel of their prayers.

Of course, this is a tradition that brings with it many challenges, and wrestling with these is part of the training of the soul in honesty. How do we cope with the apparently vengeful or militaristic psalms? What do we do with such unashamed and uninhibited anger? Can we be as honest with God, and with ourselves, about the darkness in our hearts as were the anonymous poets of these psalms? Many commentators, not least C. S. Lewis in his brilliant *Reflections on the Psalms*, have already helped us think through these issues, and readers of this book will see that in my own poetic response to the most challenging of these difficult psalms I have not shied away from the difficulty, but tackled it head-on, hoping that poetry itself can offer some new insight into praying these psalms with real honesty about ourselves and others.

For the psalms themselves are great poetry, and so rich and varied in their imagery that they feed and nourish the imagination and become a source from which our own original prayers can be formed and enriched. We pray with the psalms not simply by reciting the original text, but also by responding freely and creatively to their imagery. And this is what I have done in this new sequence of short poems, responding freely to the daily psalms and drawing on their leading images, as a starting point for Christian reflection. We recite the psalms not just as historical texts from 'out there and back then', but also as inspired words given for our own hearts to sing 'in here and right now'.

For Christians, there is the special sense that the psalms prophetically showed forth the coming of Christ, and, because they were on his lips, they give us a glimpse of his own inner life of prayer. As I say in my response to Psalm 22: 'Christ himself is crying through this psalm.' So the response I offer to the psalms here, while respecting and reflecting on their original context, is unashamedly Christian and follows the New Testament and the early church in the way they prayed the psalms in and through Christ. Which is to say that I am reading and praying the psalter in the spirit first of its having been read and prayed by Christ, and second as in some sense inspired prophecy of his inner experience, and so of my experience in him, and his in me.

My poems are neither a new translation of the psalms nor a learned commentary, but rather a contemporary prayer journal, an account of what it is like to read and pray through these ancient words now and let them speak into our own condition.

Following the example of John Donne, I have woven these poems together into a *corona*, a crown or coronet of poems, the last line of each linking to the first line of the next, and the last line of the whole sequence linking to the first, thus renewing the circle, completing the crown: a chaplet of praise to garland the head of the one who wore the *corona spinea*, the crown of thorns for us, and who has suffered with us through the corona pandemic.

Each poem is composed of 15 lines divided into five tercets in terza rima, a miniature reflection of the 150 psalms of the psalter and their traditional division. The text of the psalms to which I am responding is Coverdale's translation in the Book of Common Prayer, which also provides the traditional Latin titles I am using, and readers of this book might find it useful to read through particular psalms in that translation before turning to their corresponding poems, so as to over-hear the conversation each poem has with its original psalm. I hope, however, that this work can also be read as a poem in its own right, divided into 150 linked stanzas, taking you on a journey: from the first invitation to be rooted and fruitful, like a tree beside the waters, then through all the twists and turns of human experience. It is the experience that Christ in his humanity shares with us: the visionary glimpses of heaven, but also the sense of hellish darkness and depression; the delight in the beauties of nature and the warmth of human friendship, but also the awareness of destruction and corruption in both nature and humanity; a journey that leads down to the nadir of despair in Psalm 88, and yet recovers and continues through thick and thin, until we renew our courage and return to praise in the great doxology of the five final psalms, and come, as we did in the opening psalm, back 'to the place where every breath is praise'.

Introduction

BY PAULA GOODER

Many people will have one or more favourite psalms – those individual psalms that we return to time and time again for comfort or inspiration. Indeed, for many of us our relationship with the psalms is with individual favourites rather than with the Psalter as a whole. This is absolutely right and proper. Some psalms are clearly less inspiring than others; and we are not going to relate to them all in the same way.

However, our dependence on individual psalms means that occasionally we miss the glory of the whole. One of the many wonderful things about Malcolm Guite's poetic responses to the psalms is that they respond to the whole collection – the Psalter – from beginning to end (and then back to the beginning again). It summons us to remember that the whole collection is as important as our favourites, and that each psalm connects to other psalms and doesn't just stand on its own.

The psalms were clearly written over a number of centuries, from the reign of David all the way through to the period after the exile, which is often known as the Second Temple Period. Although it is very difficult to date some psalms with any level of certainty, as they could be talking about any period of history, others refer to very specific historic events. The most famous example of this is Psalm 137, in which weeping 'by the rivers of Babylon' refers to events that took place in the early sixth century BC. It is these specific references that suggest that, although tradition attributes them all to David, they were, in fact, written over a period of around 500 years.

It is not just individual psalms that have a life and location in history. The closer one looks at the Psalter the clearer it becomes that the whole collection had a life too. There are five collections or books of psalms within the Psalter – Psalms 1–41, 42–72, 73–89, 90–106 and 107–150. The psalms at the end of these books all contain a doxology – or section that praises God – which, though not identical in Psalms 41.13, 72.18–19, 89 and 106, all look very similar to each other. The final Psalm 150 is a doxology from beginning to end. The original five books might have been gathered together independently because there is one psalm that appears twice in the Psalter, as Psalms 14 and 53, and a few verses that are repeated (40.13–17 and 70, 60.5–12 and 108). These repetitions imply that they had already appeared in two separate books before the five books were joined to make the Psalter as a whole.

It is also interesting to notice that the tone of the collection changes as we progress through the Psalter. There are far more psalms of lament at the beginning of the Psalter and far more psalms of praise at the end – until we get to Psalm 150, which is composed entirely of praise. It is also fascinating to notice that the very middle of the Psalter in terms of verses – not in terms of psalm numbers because Psalm 119 is so long it skews where the middle comes – is Psalm 88, which is unusual in being composed entirely of lament. Every other lament psalm begins with lament but ends with a statement of praise and/or confidence in God. Psalm 88 ends: 'You have taken from me friend and neighbour – darkness is my closest friend.' In other words, it ends as gloomy as it begins – there is no light at the end of the tunnel, no hope in the darkness.

The mid-point of the Psalter is a dark place indeed but, after Psalm 88, although lament does not disappear it diminishes little by little until by Psalm 150 it has disappeared entirely. Walter Brueggemann in his various writings on the psalms draws our attention to the way in which the Psalter as a whole takes us on an emotional journey down to the pit of despair and back up again.

All in all, it is worth reading the whole Psalter from beginning to end, as well as your favourite individual psalms, and this collection of Malcolm Guite's poetic responses is a wonderful way to do it. It will guide you well as you journey from the assurance of Psalm 1, through the despair of Psalm 88 to the untrammelled joy of Psalm 150.

Psalm 1: I *Beatus vir qui non abiit*

Come to the place where every breath is praise,
And God is breathing through each passing breeze.
Be planted by the waterside and raise

Your arms with Christ beneath these rooted trees,
Who lift their breathing leaves up to the skies.
Be rooted too, as still and strong as these,

Open alike to sun and rain. Arise
From meditation by these waters. Bear
The fruit of that deep rootedness. Be wise

In the trees' long wisdom. Learn to share
The secret of their patience. Pass the day
In their green fastness and their quiet air.

Slowly discern a life, a truth, a way,
Where simple being flowers in delight.
Then let the chaff of life just blow away.

Psalm 2: II *Quare fremuerunt gentes?*

Then let the chaff of life just blow away:
The cynic scoffer and the evil troll,
The hunters and the haters who hold sway

In raging twitter storms, the ones who scroll
Through hate- and hit-lists in their tiny rage
Are dust upon the mirror of your soul.

Blow them away, the idols of this age,
And let their fury settle in the mire.
Uncap your pen and open a clean page,

For now the Lord will give you your desire
And set you high upon his holy hill.
He draws you to the garden through the fire,

Back to the fountain whence those waters spill
That christened you as his belovèd child
That you may find your peace in his good will.

Psalm 3: III *Domine, quid multiplicati?*

That you may find your peace in his good will
Call out to him, and tell him all your fear
For he will hear you from his holy hill.

He knows how many ills both far and near
Oppress your soul, and how they multiply,
These obstacles and problems, how you veer

From one side to the other, from one lie
To yet another till there's nothing true.
Just let it go for now. Don't even try.

Lie down and rest. Let him look after you,
And in the morning when you rise again
Then let him lift your head and change your view,

Replenish, renovate you, and sustain
His long slow blessings in your growing soul,
Till troubles cease and only joys remain.

Psalm 4: IV *Cum invocarem*

Till troubles cease and only joys remain
Take refuge in the shelter of his love
Who hears your call and feels with you your pain,

Who does not keep his distance, high above,
But brings his light into your little room,
Nestles and settles with you like the dove

In its familiar dovecote. From the womb
Of Mary to her house in Nazareth,
The upper chamber to the empty tomb,

He comes to share with you your every breath
And to commune with you. To every heart,
That opens to him he will bring new birth,

For every ending offer a new start.
Lie down in peace and trust and take your rest
Safe in the love of one who'll never part.

Psalm 5: V *Verba mea auribus*

Safe in the love of one who'll never part,
Of one whose kindness is itself a shield,
Who understands the deep things of my heart

Better than I can ever do, I yield
Myself and my perplexities to him,
And in his house of mercy I am healed:

Healed of this world's bloodthirstiness, its grim
Deceptions, all its weary wickedness,
The death-speak of its tyrants, as they hymn

The idols of excess, the emptiness
Of endless purchases, all washed away
Until my sight is cleansed. His righteousness

Makes my way plain, and leads me through the play
Of early morning light, to worship him
Whose mercy wakes me at the break of day.

Psalm 6: VI *Domine, ne in furore*

Whose mercy wakes me at the break of day?
I feel my weakness. All my bones are vexed
And all the faith in me seems worn away

As though I've lost love's memory. Perplexed
By false complexities, I mime faith's part.
I keep the book but cannot read the text

Unless you come, and write it in my heart,
Unless you help me read it through my tears
And hear me out, and, hearing, heal my hurt.

How could I think you punished me? My fears
Just magnified the shadows that I cast
Till you were lost in shadow too. Love hears

My cries and clears the shadows of my past
Flinging them back before his growing light
Until I recognise his face at last.

Psalm 7: VII *Domine, Deus meus*

Until I recognise his face at last
I'll trust him in the dark and carry on,
Till these destructive powers fall back to dust,

Till the devouring lions are fled and gone
Before the Great Lion's righteousness.
Then every place where some small gleam has shown

Will shine within the light of holiness,
And he will prove and make me true of heart,
My Lord and God, *Dominus deus meus.*

Evil can only break itself apart,
Recoiling back into its own destruction
And digging its own grave. It has no part

In the true kingdom. All its desolation
Will fall away to nothing and be gone,
Before the splendour of the resurrection.

Psalm 8: VIII *Domine, Dominus noster*

Before the splendour of the resurrection
Dawns and transforms the world, I'll watch the lights
Of heaven, each a glory, in their station,

Harbingers of heaven, keeping nights
Of watch with us, the moving moon and stars,
His handiwork in which he still delights.

And I will listen too: open my ears
To every creature that still speaks his name,
From babes and sucklings to those crowned with years,

For wisdom laughs and lives in both. The flame
Of love is kindled round the world in old
And young. I'll seek him too beyond the tame

Familiar world, out in the wide and wild,
As much in the steep seas, and mountain heights
As in the startling wisdom of a child.

Psalm 9: IX *Confitebor tibi*

As in the startling wisdom of a child,
So also in remembering the poor
Our scales are readjusted, reconciled

To the true calibrations that endure
When God in all his justice holds those scales,
Redresses our imbalance and his sure

And steadfast covenant at last prevails.
And even now I will rejoice in him,
Now, when it sometimes seems that goodness fails

My song will still delight in his good name.
So come and join the song, daughters of Albion,
Come and rejoice with all whom he calls home

Rejoice through every age and stage and aeon
As, patiently abiding with the meek,
We sing with all the daughters of true Sion.

Psalm 10: X *Ut quid, Domine?*

We sing with all the daughters of true Sion
But now our song must be a rebel song:
A song against the proud devouring lion,

A song that cries aloud, O Lord, how long?
How long will you stand back and let them be
These vicious tricksters, thinking they're so strong,

Who make a boast of their own vanity;
Capricious 'leaders' feeding their desire
For self-aggrandisement, whose idiocy

Sickens the nations that they should inspire.
They care for nothing but themselves, and say
That God will never see it. They retire

Onto their yachts and golf-courses, where they
Still mock the people they oppress. Arise
Arise, my God, and give the poor their day!

Psalm 11: XI *In Domino confido*

Arise, my God, and give the poor their day!
For now I see the powers taking aim
And targeting the weakest. See, they slay

The true of heart and still they falsely claim
To be our shepherds! Where then can I fly?
I envy birds their wings, but sorrows maim,

And my complicities constrain me. I
Desire with all my soul to seek the hill
Where God has set his citadel on high.

Through all these sad constraints I trust him still;
I know that he can see the way things go
I know that these dark ways are not his will

For he loves justice, and the poor will know
That he is their defender when he comes
To topple tyrants and exalt the low.

Psalm 12: XII *Salvum me fac*

To topple tyrants and exalt the low,
Up, Lord, and help us! Hear our hapless sighs.
We have been cowed by 'people in the know'.

The worldly wind us in a web of lies.
We have been flattered into servitude,
Snared with devices that the rich devise.

They purchase us with their fake plenitude,
They keep us clicking on false images.
The one percent controls the multitude

With slick distractions, online purchases,
Whose icons all prove idols in the end.
They market us as passive packages.

Send us instead your pure words, Jesus, send
Us hope, still silver-bright, tried in the fire,
Come down to free us, come as our true friend.

Psalm 13: XIII *Usque quo, Domine?*

Come down to free us, come as our true friend,
How long, how long? Oh do not hide your face
Or let me sleep in death, but light my end,

Till it becomes a bright beginning. Place
Your wounded hands in mine and raise me up
That even grief itself may turn to grace.

Then I will sing a song of sudden hope,
Then I will praise my saviour, the divine
Companion who drank the bitter cup

And in so doing made it flow with wine,
That his strong love might overrun my heart
And all his joy in heaven might be mine.

Then I will sing his song, and take my part
In Love's true music, as his kingdom comes
And heaven's hidden gates are drawn apart.

Psalm 14: XIV *Dixit insipiens*

When heaven's hidden gates are drawn apart
And our captivity is ended, we'll rejoice,
But now the fool's in charge, and in his heart

He only echoes his own emptiness:
No god, no vestiges of reverence
Disturb his vanity. Just weariness

And mockery, just cruel insolence,
And greed that still consumes the poor like bread,
These only seem to move him. Violence

Is like a drug to him. He cocks his head
And speaks his poison words with hissing tongue
And yet we still believe him. Let him dread

The day that's coming, it will not be long.
The poor have cried, and now they have been heard
The fool will fall before their joyful song.

Psalm 15: XV *Domine, quis habitabit?*

The fool will fall before their joyful song
But maybe I will fall with him as well.
You know me, Lord, you know how much I long

To rise with you, how much I long to dwell
Within your tabernacle, to ascend
The path that glimmers on your holy hill,

But you know too how much I just pretend
To virtues not my own. I am not fit
For that ascent. I fail unless you lend

Your strength and take my life and make of it
A new life altogether. Oh descend
Into my darkness, lift me from the pit

And set me on the way that you intend,
How ever slow and spiralling the path
Then help me, step by step, my guide and friend.

Psalm 16: XVI *Conserva me, Domine*

Then help me, step by step, my guide and friend.
Preserve me O my God in whom I trust.
My other goods are nothing in the end.

How quickly they decay, how swiftly rust!
But through it all you stay and comfort me,
My one abiding joy, when all the rest

Have flown so suddenly. For now I see
My true inheritance, now I look up
And find you still beside me, showing me

The path of life. In your right hand the cup
Of blessings full to overflowing. Your
Left hand upholds me still, and gives me hope.

I have a goodly heritage! You pour
On me your graces, undeserved, you raise
And comfort me until I fall no more.

Psalm 17: XVII *Exaudi, Domine*

Oh comfort me until I fall no more.
In this dark season when I am so frail
And fearful, comfort me. I stand before

You in your house at evening. I avail
Myself of compline's long familiar chant
To call on you. I ask you to prevail

Over the powers that dull and disenchant,
Over the scoffing of a world that's steeped
In its own excess, and instead to plant

Me firmly by your waters, and to keep
Me as the apple of an eye, to hide
Me in the shadow of your wings. I'll sleep

In peace and take my rest. I will abide
In your rich presence now, and when I wake
I will behold you, and be satisfied.

Psalm 18: XVIII *Diligam te, Domine*

I will behold you, and be satisfied,
My strength, my rock, my buckler, and my shield!
You came to rescue me, I saw you ride

The wind's swift wings, I saw the waters yield
To you, as you reached down to lift me out
Out of the whelming panic, where I reeled

And flailed in fear of death. You heard my shout,
My anguished cry for help, and carried me
And held me safe and put my fears to rout.

And now you give me back my liberty,
You strengthen my weak hands and set my feet
To dancing lightly as a deer, as free

As any in the forest, and as fleet.
Soon you will call and draw me in your love
To that still place where earth and heaven meet.

Psalm 19: XIX *Caeli enarrant*

In that still place where earth and heaven meet
Under mysterious starlight, raise your head
And gaze up at their glory: 'the complete

Consort dancing' as one poet said
Of his own words. But these are all God's words:
A shining poem, waiting to be read

Afresh in every heart. Now look towards
The bright'ning east, and see the splendid sun
Rise and rejoice, the icon of his Lord's

True light. Be joyful with him, watch him run
His course, receive the treasure of his light
Pouring like honeyed gold till day is done,

As sweet and strong as all God's laws, as right
As all his judgements and as clean and pure,
All given for your growth, and your delight!

Psalm 20: XX *Exaudiat te Dominus*

All given for your growth, and your delight,
All flowing for you from his sanctuary.
Even before you enter in, his light

Is blessing you. Now may his mystery
Still draw you on, arouse your heart's desire,
And may each glimpse become epiphany.

May brief sparks blaze into a holy fire
Whose light and warmth illuminate your mind.
And may some scent and sense of heav'n inspire

Your thoughts and words. May everything remind
You of your Lord, that you may put your trust
Entirely in his name, not in the blind

Dependence of this world, whose weapons rust
Into the soul and kill it from within.
But may you find in Christ, riches *and* rest.

Psalm 21: XXI *Domine, in virtute tua*

Now may you find in Christ, riches *and* rest,
May you be blessed in him, and he in you
In Heaven, where to grant you your request

Is always blessing, for your heart is true:
True to yourself and true to Christ your king.
Breathe through this coronation psalm and view

The glory of his golden crown, then sing
The exaltation, goodness, life and power,
The blessing and salvation Christ will bring.

But first he wears a darker crown. The hour
Is coming and has come. Our Lord comes down
Into the heart of all our hurts to wear

The sharp *corona spinea*, crown
Of thorns, and to descend with us to death
Before he shares with us the golden crown.

Psalm 22: XXII *Deus, Deus meus*

Before he shares with us the golden crown,
He comes to share with us the crown of thorns.
Our hurts and hates close in and hem him round

Mock and humiliate him. All the scorns
With which we blaspheme God in one another
Are concentrated here among 'the horns

Of unicorns', the lions' mouths, the slather
Of our devouring wickedness. He takes
It all and turns it into love. He gathers

All of us and by atonement makes
Our peace with God. He speaks to us of mercy
Even as we pierce him. No-one slakes

His thirst. I tremble at the mystery
For Christ himself is crying through this psalm,
To suffer my own dereliction for me.

Psalm 23: XXIII *Dominus regit me*

To suffer my own dereliction for me,
To be my shepherd, and to lead me through
The grave and gate of death, in strength and mercy

Christ has come down. At last I've found the true
Shepherd and the false just fade away
Before him. I will sing of how he drew

Me from the snares I set myself, how day
Dawned on my darkness, how he brought me forth,
Converted me and opened up the way

For me, and led me gently on that path,
Led me beside still waters, promised me
That he'd be with me all my days on earth,

And when my last day comes, accompany
And comfort me, as evening shadows fall,
And draw me into his eternity.

Psalm 24: XXIV *Domini est terra*

And draw me into his eternity?
But who can rise up to that holy place?
Can all its splendours really be for me?

Before that holy fire I hide my face.
My hands were never clean, as for my heart
He'll search out its impurity and trace

The sources of its sin in every part,
And in the whole, its weariness and stain.
Who can ascend? I cannot even start.

But even as I fear my hopes are vain
My saviour comes, his love revives my hope.
I feel him search my wounds, deal with my pain,

And offer me again the healing cup.
Raising my head, he says: 'Now rise with me
The gates will open for us both, look up!'

Psalm 25: XXV *Ad te, Domine, levavi*

The gates will open for us both, look up!
I hear that voice each day when I'm downcast.
I hear it when I've almost lost my hope,

And now, when I'm entangled by my past,
My feet are netted by necessity,
Snared in the traps of time that bind so fast,

My eyes turned downward, dimmed by what they see,
I hear that voice again and raise my eyes
As he untangles me and sets me free.

He alters my perspective. The wide skies
Speak of his mercy, and the distant hills
Stand in his steadfast love and make me wise

In his simplicity, and all my ills
Diminish and recede to their true size,
That I may find my peace in all he wills.

Psalm 26: XXVI *Judica me, Domine*

That I may find my peace in all he wills
I call on him in faith, to judge for me,
Since my own judgement fails and all my skills

In reckoning forget his clemency.
For when I judge myself, when I judge others
I do so with a false severity.

He has a far more patient love, that gathers
His lost and fallen children, brings them home
Into that habitation where he mothers,

Fathers, and befriends us, where the same
Love is lavished on the least as on
The greatest and he welcomes all who come

To him. I may have shunned them, but the son
Who died for them knows better than I do,
Oh let me see with his eyes from now on!

Psalm 27: XXVII *Dominus illuminatio*

Oh let me see with his eyes from now on
Whose gaze on beauty makes it beautiful,
Who looks us into love and looks upon

His whole creation with a merciful
And loving eye. My heart has said of him
Seek out his face, I've sensed his bountiful

Presence shimmering behind the dim
Veil of things. That presence calls to me,
Calls me to tremble at the brink and rim

Of lived experience, and then to free
Myself of fear, to trust him, and to dive
Right off that brink, into his mystery,

Into that deep and holy sea of love
In which the living worlds all float and swim,
To dare each moment's death, that I might live.

Psalm 28: XXVIII *Ad te, Domine*

To dare each moment's death, that I might live
Means both repentance and a plenitude
Of grace, means letting go to let him give.

So Christ I beg for that beatitude:
The grace to trust and let go, to receive
From your unsparing hand the amplitude

Of your beneficence, to have a heart
That dances to the measure of your music
Even here where evil seeks to part

Us from each promised good, and where the sick
And sickening cacophony of hate
Might deafen us or wound us to the quick

And break us down. May it not be too late
To turn to you again and start to live,
Call us, O Christ, and open up the gate.

Psalm 29: XXIX *Afferte Domino*

Call us, O Christ, and open up the gate.
Call us to worship with your mighty voice:
The voice that sings through rivers in full spate,

The voice in which the forests all rejoice,
The voice that rolls through thunderclouds, and calls
The deep seas and steep waves, the quiet voice

That stirs our sleeping conscience and recalls
Us to the love we had abandoned, leads
Us through the parting mists of doubt, or falls

Upon us like a revelation, pleads
With us upon the poor's behalf, blazes
In glory from each burning bush, and bleeds

Out from compassion's wounds, the voice that raises
Our drooping spirits till we dance for joy
And gives us too, a voice to sing his praises.

Psalm 30: XXX *Exaltabo te, Domine*

He gives us too, a voice to sing his praises,
So much the more because we were brought low
That we might know we have a God who raises

Up the lowly. Riches made us slow
To love you, slow to turn to you in praise
But sudden loss and crisis made us know

Our true dependence on your love. Our days
Of false security are gone. We fell
Into a pit of our own making. Raise

Us up again, each out of our own hell,
And give us oil for ashes, joy for mourning.
Restore us in your love and we will tell

Of how through our long night we heard your warning
And heeded you, and found your love again,
How night withdrew and joy came in the morning.

Psalm 31: XXXI *In te, Domine, speravi*

The night withdrew and joy came in the morning,
When I remembered that I was remembered,
That even through the bitter tears of mourning

I was sustained. The darkest powers were hindered
In their insidious work within my soul,
And I was held together and re-membered

By your unceasing love. You made me whole
When all the world was tearing me apart.
When there was fear on every side, you stole

Into the secret garden of my heart,
A good thief in the night, and hid with me
In your strong tabernacle, held apart

From all that strife of tongues, cacophony
Of condemnations, so you kept me safe
In your deep silence and your mystery.

Psalm 32: XXXII *Beati, quorum*

In your deep silence and your mystery
You led me to confess and be forgiven,
You gave me the relief of honesty.

How long and bitterly I might have striven
With all the guilt that I could hardly name,
How painfully my heart might have been riven

By hidden memories and secret shame.
Instead you blessed me with a new beginning,
Unbound me from the bands and brands of blame,

My false accounts of losing or of winning,
And called me to come forth like Lazarus
And start my life again, rejoicing, singing,

Baptised and born in your mysterious
And all-involving love, a love that lifts,
A love that comforts and embraces us.

Psalm 33: XXXIII *Exultate, justi*

A love that comforts and embraces us
Is the true theme of every song I make:
How tenderly he finds and places us

Deep into Christ himself for his love's sake.
The strings of all my instruments will stir
My heart to praise. Therefore I rise and take

My harp, my mandolin, my old guitar,
And let them sound a new song in his praise,
Whose word is true, whose works so full and fair,

Are radiant with glory, and whose ways
Are tried and trusted. Every ounce of earth
Is charged and brimming with his goodness. Days

Are all ordained to praise him; by his breath
The stars of night are kindled; by his love
He raises and delivers us from death.

Psalm 34: XXXIV *Benedicam Domino*

He raises and delivers us from death,
And even now he shows us how to live
That we might savour life with every breath,

That we might taste and see, might truly thrive,
Might see the good days that he wants for us
And make the best of all he has to give.

And so he comes to live as one of us
And teaches us afresh the ways of peace.
He lives the fullest life in front of us

And shows us how to break the bonds, release
The captive, seek the truth that sets us free,
To choose the right and do it, to increase

The reach of love, the possibility
Of fruitful life together, and to hear
The poor cry out and help them speedily.

Psalm 35: XXXV *Judica, Domine*

The poor cry out, Oh help them speedily
And plead their cause, though it may not be mine.
The psalmist here is sure in crying 'help *me*'!

But he was poor himself. Help me divine
How these sharp psalms call out for change in me
Lest I should be an 'enemy of thine',

And find the poor, who cry to you for mercy,
Have cried against me too! Oh let me not
Be numbered with these scoffers, Lord, convert me,

Show me with whom I ought to share my lot,
For whom I ought to put the sackcloth on,
Whom you remember, whom I have forgot,

That having wept with them and helped them on
To better things, we may rejoice together
As pilgrim souls on whom your light has shone.

Psalm 36: XXXVI *Dixit injustus*

As pilgrim souls on whom your light has shone
Let us leave judgement to your tender mercy
And turn instead to you, keep pressing on

Towards the steadfast heights, the mountain country
Of your holy presence. Let us drink
From your swift river, our true ecstasy.

Refresh us Christ, and bring us to the brink
Of that deep well where life itself is light,
And goodness, more than we can dream or think,

Flows from your plenteousness, from your delight
In all your works, and where your loving-kindness
Shines through our day and comforts us at night,

Like soft wings safely overarching us,
That we might put our utter trust in you
And fret no more for passing wickedness.

Psalm 37: XXXVII *Noli aemulari*

I'll fret no more for passing wickedness,
No more than for the new-mown grass that fades
To leave room for the growth and tenderness

Of fresh green leaves; the cool inviting glades
Of my new life in you, my heart's desire.
The True Sun rises now, and soon the shades,

The last black shades of night, will 'back retire
And mix no more with good'. Then I will sing
The song of my redemption in that choir

Where I, whom you have made, at last can bring
My song to its beginning and its end.
Till then I'll be content with each small thing

Your love provides, and let the rich contend
With one another for their fading wealth,
For I have found my God and my true friend.

Psalm 38: XXXVIII *Domine, ne in furore*

For I have found my God and my true friend,
And heaven knows I need his friendship now.
For I am weak, my days draw to an end

Or so it seems to me. I sigh and bow
My head in bitterness. The stress and strain
Of chronic illnesses have laid me low.

How can I praise you when I roar with pain?
Smitten with affliction and infection,
No sooner soothed than in distress again,

And made more bitter by the sad reflection
That half of this I brought down on my head
In folly. I deserve my dereliction,

My portion of disquietness and dread.
Forsake me not, O Lord my God, make haste,
Deliver me and raise me from the dead!

Psalm 39: XXXIX *Dixi, custodiam*

Deliver me and raise me from the dead
For I have walked in shadows. Nothingness,
The vanity of things, fills me with dread,

The sheer inanity, the pointlessness
Of how we used to live – we can't go back
To that – the rush that masked our emptiness,

All the pretence that covered what we lack,
When what we really lacked was always you.
I held my tongue, but I could see the crack

In everything we build and say and do.
And now the crack is widening. I pray
That we will turn and see a light break through

These fissures that so fill us with dismay.
The death we fear is birth, the shell is breaking:
The stone itself will soon be rolled away.

Psalm 40: XL *Expectans expectavi*

The stone itself will soon be rolled away.
I wait in patience, all expectantly,
Firm on this rock above the miry clay

Where he has set me in his loving mercy.
I sing my psalm in Christ who sings in me,
A new song made in his Love's mystery:

'Your wondrous works all rise like wings in me
And lift my heart to praise. I hear your call,
The simple call of Love: *Oh come to me!*

Bring me no gifts, for I have made them all,
Just bring yourself, and open up your heart.'
And so I come to you and bring you all,

All that I am and have been: joy and hurt,
Glory and shame. I bring you everything,
That you might make me whole in every part.

Psalm 41: XLI *Beatus qui intelligit*

That you might make me whole in every part,
Have mercy on me now. Oh raise me up
And comfort me when things just fall apart.

For you have known this too: the grip and grope
Of suffering, the time when comforts fail,
The cruel pretence of friendship, the false hope

Of some relief, the sense of being frail,
Of being helpless, wounded, vulnerable,
And worst of all the sickening betrayal

By those we thought were closest, miserable
Dependence on the ones who've lost our trust.
What can I do but cry 'be merciful,

Be merciful and raise me from the dust.
Restore my health, because I cry to you,
You are my heart's desire from first to last'.

Psalm 42: XLII *Quemadmodum*

You are my heart's desire from first to last
Like as the hart desires the water brooks
So longs my soul towards you. So I thirst

For living streams, not for the dusty books
They write about you, nor the empty words
That ring from pulpits, nor the haughty looks

Of those who market you. These are the shards
Of broken idols. I long for the deep
In you that calls the deep in me, the chords

That sound those depths and summon me to weep
At first with tears of grief and then with tears
Of joy, that I may sow those tears and reap

A timeless harvest, that the ripened ears
Of grain may shine as clean and clear as gold
Shucked of the husk of all my wasted years.

Psalm 43: XLIII *Judica me, Deus*

Shucked of the husk of all my wasted years,
I long to step forth, free of all encumbrance,
To set aside the heaviness, the tears,

The sin that clings so close, the doleful hindrance
Of resentment and regret, to let them go,
Roll them below the cross, as Christian once

Did in his pilgrim's progress. Then I'd know
A lighter step once more; the joy and gladness
The psalmist longs for here. Oh Jesus, show

Me once again the path out of my sadness
And set my steps back on your holy hill.
Send out your light and truth to be my witness,

And since I cannot climb by my own will,
Abide with me and be my will, my strength,
The living fountain whence I drink my fill.

Psalm 44: XLIV *Deus, auribus*

The living fountain whence I drink my fill,
Must rise in me before I sing this psalm.
How could it ever be God's Holy will

To raise an army, to inflict the harm,
The special horror of a holy war?
How could we ever conquer in his name?

O Jesus, did you sing this psalm before
You girded strength to brave your agony,
To fight the only holy battle for

The world you loved, and heal the misery
Of all mankind? As for us you were smitten
Into the place of dragons, victory

Was won for all of us, as it is written
And so in Christ shall all be made alive
And still we live as if we have forgotten.

Psalm 45: XLV *Eructavit cor meum*

And still we live as if we have forgotten,
But someone keeps all these things in her heart.
She bore for us the only one begotten,

The Son of God, and now she takes our part
And calls us to remember all his mercy,
Calls us with all our skill, and all our art

To magnify his name, for it is holy.
For now she dwells with him, in joy and gladness,
The Mystic Rose of heaven, once so lowly

Whose heart was also pierced, who feels our sadness
And shows us how to pray. Each generation
Has known her help and presence, heard her witness

The great things done through her. In every nation
She nurtures those who bear Christ to the world.
Through her our saviour came, Love's revelation.

Psalm 46: XLVI *Deus noster refugium*

Through her our saviour came, Love's revelation.
For God was in the midst of her, and now
We too are called, in every generation

To find in him our hope and strength, although
The busy world around us falls apart,
And all our towering schemes have been laid low.

Now is the time to take his truth to heart
And to be glad within the holy place
That he himself has made in us, to start

Each day with him, abiding in his grace
As he abides with us, to know his peace,
To turn towards his light and seek his face,

To let his loving spirit find release
And flow through us into his weary world,
That wrongs may be redressed and wars may cease.

Psalm 47: XLVII *Omnes gentes, plaudite*

That wrongs may be redressed and wars may cease
He must be king of earth as well as heaven.
We must invite him here, to make his peace

Within us and between us, that forgiven,
We may release forgiveness here on earth,
Working and spreading like a holy leaven;

A secret of the kingdom; Heaven's breath;
A kindling from the place where Christ is king.
For he has triumphed and defeated death

And even now he calls our hearts to sing:
Sing praises in the kingdom still to come
And in the one already here, to bring

Ourselves, our arts and music, trumpet, drum
And tabor, all to make a merry noise,
For heaven's king has made the earth his home!

Psalm 48: XLVIII *Magnus Dominus*

For heaven's king has made the earth his home,
Not just the hill of Sion, but the whole
Round world. From anywhere you call to him

He'll come to you and make his dwelling. Hail
Your God in any language, he replies
In your own mother-tongue. For now your soul

Is his true Sion, and each day you rise
Already in the city of your God.
So mark the towers and turrets, and apprise

Again the beauty of your new abode.
Your soul is greater than you ever knew:
Walk round its walls, then take the holy road

That winds towards its centre, where the new
Temple of his spirit shines and stands,
Where Christ himself is there to welcome you.

Psalm 49: XLIX *Audite haec, omnes*

Where Christ himself is there to welcome you
Then you are home, wherever you may fare.
And Christ will keep your inner compass true

Though all the world is rushing everywhere,
This way and that before the winds of fear,
Between false hopes and premature despair.

But you can hear a different tune. You hear
The strong song of his love. Open your ears
To hear his parables. The foolish veer

Between their fatuous desires and fears,
With fickle fortunes that they fear to share.
Keep your security in Christ, who hears

The slightest murmur of your smallest prayer,
And do not be afraid, but trust in him,
Your heart's in heaven, keep your treasure there.

Psalm 50: L *Deus deorum*

Your heart's in heaven, keep your treasure there,
For Heaven itself is coming to the earth!
Our God is coming, and he will appear

In perfect beauty. All these pangs of birth
Will turn to joy as our whole world is born
Again in him. The pain, the want, the dearth,

The dark, will vanish in that rising dawn,
And all the creatures on a thousand hills:
People and beasts and birds, that holy morn,

Will join in one dawn chorus. Glory spills
Already from beneath that glad horizon
And even now you hear his voice. He calls

You through your conscience, calls you through your reason,
He calls you through your deep imagination
He calls you to discern his time and season.

Psalm 51: LI *Miserere mei, Deus*

He calls you to discern his time and season.
The sempiternal season of his mercy
Lifts like the sun above your dark horizon.

Expose your darkness, sing your *miserere,*
His light will judge, and judging, heal your sin.
Then bathe in sheer beauty, as Allegri

Sounds out your penitence, and let Christ clean
Your soul once more, erasing every stain
Washing you thoroughly. For he has seen

What you confess and what you hide. Again
He mends your broken bones and makes for you
A clean heart, comes to comfort you again,

Comes with his Holy Spirit to renew
The spirit in you, calling you to sing
Of all your loving God has done for you.

Psalm 52: LII *Quid gloriaris?*

Of all your loving God has done for you,
Of all his many mercies on your soul,
Surely the greatest was his planting you

Like a green olive tree, secure and whole,
To grow within his holy house forever.
Be rooted once again in the rich soil

Of his deep love, and know that none can sever,
No power on earth can ever separate
You from the steadfast love of Christ your saviour.

So let the tyrants boast. Their desperate
Endeavours to maintain their godless power
Will come to nothing soon, evaporate

Like morning mist before the sun. The hour
Is coming and has come. Their time is up,
But you will flourish in God's house forever.

Psalm 53: LIII *Dixit insipiens*

Though we will flourish in God's house forever,
We live within a world that counts him out
Of every calculation, one that never

Considers that it might be wrong. No doubt
Can pierce our presumption. We dismiss
The wisdom of the past, and yet we flout

The principle of open-mindedness,
Presuming from the start on our conclusion.
That cast of mind has cast a spell on us:

A spell of disenchantment, the illusion
That only matter matters. Break the spell,
Lord Jesus, and undo our dark confusion,

Deliver us again, remove the veil,
The thin familiar film that covers wonder,
Let us rejoice to see your light prevail.

Psalm 54: LIV *Deus, in nomine*

Let us rejoice to see your light prevail
Save us O God! For what the tyrants seek
Is not our bodies but our very soul!

The freedom of the heart is now at stake.
The enemies of freedom are within
Each one of us, for we have let them speak

With our own voices, magnified the din
Of blasphemous cacophony. We've used
Our own devices to embed our sin,

'Distracted from distraction', and confused
By dark diversions of our own devising.
Each gift of yours has somehow been abused

To cast doubt on the giver, by revising
The tenets of our faith, till they're half dead.
Oh rouse and raise us, in your Easter rising!

Psalm 55: LV *Exaudi, Deus*

Oh rouse and raise us, in your Easter rising.
Darkness and fear are coming on so fast
And with such open malice, still devising

Their mischief for the faithful. The clenched fist
Is raised once more against the open hand.
I fear to lose my power to resist.

Oh hear my prayer and heed me, help me stand
Steadfast in the stronghold of your love.
Give me the strength and courage to withstand

These onslaughts on my soul. Help me forgive
The bitter wounds of personal betrayal.
Give me those wings indeed, wings of a dove,

Not to retreat, but rise within the veil
And rest awhile in you and be at peace
Assured once more that goodness will prevail.

Psalm 56: LVI *Miserere mei, Deus*

Assured once more that goodness will prevail,
I praise you for your Word, and trust in you,
Take up my part in the unfinished tale

Of Jesus' risen life, once more renew
My little role within the coming kingdom.
And though I am afraid, Lord, keep me true,

Keep me from giving in, and from the thraldom
Of all this present darkness, from its slave
Mentality and weariness. Your wisdom

Glimmers in me still, sustain and save
Me in your love. You know too well my fears,
My fretful flittings back and forth. Oh lave

And bathe me in your cleansing love, that tears
Themselves might be a balm, until the day
Of our salvation dawns, and Christ appears.

Psalm 57: LVII *Miserere mei, Deus*

Until salvation dawns, and Christ appears,
Until this tyranny be overpast,
Your wings will cover us and calm our fears.

So fix our hearts upon the joys that last,
That even though we walk amidst the fire,
Where threats and taunts and curses are still cast

To drag us down, instead we will rise higher
In your great mercy, lifted into heaven,
The mountain country of the heart's desire,

The country where our sins are all forgiven.
And there we'll sing and praise you every morning.
Though darkness still dwells here, the clouds are riven

By lightning strikes of grace. Though here I'm mourning,
Already in your kingdom my heart dances,
And even here I'll sing, for day is dawning.

Psalm 58: LVIII *Si vere utique*

And even here I'll sing, for day is dawning,
Although I know some of my deeds are dark.
The psalmist asks hard questions, and the yawning

Gap between my prayer and practice, work
And words, has been exposed in scripture's light.
Where have I set my mind? How do I shirk

The good work he has given me? The right
Way is always open, do I follow?
Or do I stop my ears? Or make some slight

Progress at a snail's pace, all my hollow
Protestations shown for what they are
Even as I make them? Come and hallow

My broken ground again, come and repair
The ruin of my efforts to do well,
The breach between my practice and my prayer.

Psalm 59: LIX *Eripe me de inimicis*

The breach between my practice and my prayer
Exposes me to malice both without
And deep within. I'm only too aware

That I can't pray this psalm, without some doubt
That I myself might be amongst the ones
Who run around the walls with greedy snout

And grudge if they're not satisfied. My groans
In prayer to you are sometimes nothing more
Than my own dog's desire for juicy bones.

Deliver me, O Lord, and show me your
Patience and your mercy, set me free
Not from the sins of others, or the score

I sometimes keep of their iniquity,
But from my own deep-seated faults and flaws,
From my false self, O Lord, deliver me.

Psalm 60: LX *Deus, repulisti nos*

From my false self, O Lord, deliver me.
Where I am scattered gather me again,
Turn me to you once more, and turn to me,

For we have all been shaken. Soothe our pain
And heal the deep divisions, cruelly shown
By this sharp plague. All other help is vain,

So be our help. Our future's all unknown
To us. We trust that you will meet us there,
Since all of time is in your hands, all known

And carried in your providence. Our prayer
Rises from every land, from Gillead
From Succoth, from New York, from places where

Your other names are spoken. All the sad
And sighing tribes of earth hold up their hands:
Hear us, we cry, and once more, make us glad.

Psalm 61: LXI *Exaudi, Deus*

Hear us, we cry, and once more, make us glad
From every corner of the earth we call.
From heavy hearts, from weary souls and sad

Our cry ascends towards your holy hill:
Oh lift us up and set us on the rock,
On something higher than our wavering will,

And free us from the traps of time: the clock
That counts us down to nothing, the false hope,
The game-plan and trajectory, the lock

That closes out your grace. Help us look up
And see the shimmer of the angels' wings
And, in between the cherubim, the cup

Of our salvation, and the king of kings
Come down to share himself in bread and wine.
Draw back the veil until our spirit sings.

Psalm 62: LXII *Nonne Deo?*

Draw back the veil until my spirit sings
And teach me how to wait upon your Word,
Content beneath the shadow of your wings,

Gathering strength in you, until I've heard
The Word that sends me back into the world
With all its tottering walls, with all its scarred

And ruined landscapes, ragged flags unfurled,
Its broken promises, and compromises,
The world you love and suffer for, the world

You lift to God, the world that still devises
Its own destruction, in its vanity
Selling its living soul for passing prizes.

I am to love this world as tenderly
As you do, to risk everything for love,
For love lifts time into eternity.

Psalm 63: LXIII *Deus, Deus meus*

For love lifts time into eternity,
Kisses each passing moment into life,
Gives us a glimpse of your unfading glory.

We fall away like every falling leaf
But even as we fall we yearn for you.
Our prayers are passing and our blessings brief,

Yet each one reaches deeply into you
For you yourself are reaching into us
To breathe your life in us and make us new;

The barren wasteland is made glorious
With blossoms, breathing an eternal spring
And even as this first world fades from us,

We step into the true world and we sing
A joyful song, for there at last we see
Our heart's desire: our risen Lord and King.

Psalm 64: LXIV *Exaudi, Deus*

Our hearts desire our risen Lord and King,
In our long exile here we call to him:
'Preserve us, hide us, hold us in the ring

Of your protecting love. For there are grim
Assailants round us, setting secret snares.
And when our lights are low, our vision dim

We tumble into trouble unawares
As this world's traps and trappings snag our feet.
We stumble, all encumbered by its cares,

And soon the arrows pierce us; we retreat
From our first faith, we veer and compromise,
Despair of progress and accept defeat.

Hear us and rescue us. O Lord, arise,
Shoot back for us with flaming darts of truth
And in your shining wisdom, make us wise'.

Psalm 65: LXV *Te decet hymnus*

Lord, in your shining wisdom, make us wise.
Morning and evening turn to you in praise,
Your glory stands where steadfast mountains rise.

Your presence girds us like the sea. The days
Arrive as gifts from you. The starlit nights
All manifest the beauty of your ways.

Your love touches the earth itself, alights
Not just in rain and growth and plenteousness
Or in the crowning goodness, which delights

The eye at harvest, but you visit us
And bless us far more deeply in your Son
Who came, a grain of wheat, sown deep for us

Into the furrowed grave, planted alone
That we might die and rise again with him
In the rich valley of the resurrection.

Psalm 66: LXVI *Jubilate Deo*

In the rich valley of the resurrection
The *jubilate deo* will resound
A jubilant rejoicing in perfection.

But even here the echo of that sound
Of perfect praise enriches our brief song,
A canticle that's taken up around

The world. The voices of the weak are strong
In God's enduring praise. He knows their cause,
And he will vindicate the poor, who long

To see his justice come and his good laws
Prevail at last. Till then their jubilation
Will shake the powers that be and give them pause

To tremble in the midst of exploitation
And glimpse in others all the joy they've missed,
Till love himself comes as a revelation.

Psalm 67: LXVII *Deus misereatur*

Till love himself comes as a revelation
We'll live on mercy, and we'll seek his face
Whose every look is light. In every nation

He is acknowledged, and all peoples trace
The shimmer of his presence, seek to follow
The hints and glimmers of his fleeting grace,

Feel after him and find him, learn to hallow
The places where the veil seems very thin:
The forest grove at sunrise or the hollow

In the hills on autumn evenings when
We seem to hear the horns of Efland blowing
And strange unearthly longings draw us in.

Then we come close to God without our knowing,
As he approaches us with wordless blessing,
And Eden's rivers here on earth are flowing.

Psalm 68: LXVIII *Exurgat Deus*

And Eden's rivers here on earth are flowing,
Invisibly they rise within our hearts,
Springs in the wilderness to keep us going,

Balm on our bruises, healing of our hurts.
We lie amongst the broken shards, and yet
You have not left us comfortless: our hearts

Are stirred to life, and over us you set
Your spirit like a dove with silver wings
And golden feathers. All her stirrings let

In the light of heaven. When she sings
Our spirits lift and blossom in her song
And praise the mighty JAH who made all things.

Grace of the graceful, true strength of the strong,
The captor of captivity, his day
Is coming, and the time will not be long.

Psalm 69: LXIX *Salvum me fac*

His day is coming, it will not be long!
But first he came to suffer with us here.
That sorrow might yet tremble into song,

The psalmist here foresees and counts each tear
Our saviour weeps, sees how he was accused
So falsely, sees the spite, the shame, the fear

Surrounding him, the way he was abused
By those he came to save, the way his zeal
Was mocked and taunted, mercy was refused.

And all this was for me, that he might seal
Me in the book of life, not raze me out.
They cried for vengeance, but he came to heal.

Christ takes this psalm and turns it inside out
He does not pour out indignation, but
Instead pours out the life-blood of his heart.

Psalm 70: LXX *Deus in adjutorium*

Pour out for me the life-blood of your heart
For my own life is ebbing to a close.
Make haste to help me, come and heal my hurt,

Come down, O Lord, and rescue me from those
Who seek to sow confusion in my soul,
From those who patronise the faithful, those

Who humour our religion, but whose whole
Approach to life dismisses faith and prayer.
Yet you continue holy. You will heal

The deep wounds in our culture: its despair,
Its idols and addictions, its rejection
Of your gospel. In your mercy spare

This weary world, descending to dejection,
And come as our redeemer, quickly come
And raise us with you in your resurrection.

Psalm 71: LXXI *In te, Domine, speravi*

You raise us with you in your resurrection
If we will only let you. So, Lord, come
Deliver me, and raise me from dejection

Then lift me to your stronghold. Let your name
Be my delight and my protection. Call
Me once again, and kindle love to flame.

For you have been my only hope in all
My days of life. You are the saviour who
Drew me from my mother's womb, when all

Around me gave me up for dead. But you
Inspired the nurse who nursed me back to life,
Back in Ibadan all those years ago.

And now in age I open a new leaf
In my life's manuscript and write for you
Another psalm to praise your light and life.

Psalm 72: LXXII *Deus, judicium*

Another psalm to praise your light and life
Another song of longing for the King
Who is to come, whose coming ends all strife,

Who will defend the poor, descend and bring
With him the saints in glory and a new
Heaven and Earth. And then those saints will sing

Their triumph song, and all that's tried and true
Will live again beyond the reach of death.
Yet he has come already, like the dew

Upon the grass, borne on the quiet breath
Of God's own spirit, Christ the saviour came
To Bethlehem, like rain on the good earth

And those who met his love and learned his name
Became like him and kept this hope alive
That one day the whole world would live in him.

Psalm 73: LXXIII *Quam bonus Israel!*

Though one day the whole world will live in him
The story of his saving love began
In Israel and still we honour them,

The prophets of the coming Son of Man
Whose poetry and scriptures form our mind,
As with this psalmist, sharing all his pain,

His doubts and his frustrations. For we find
That all his old misgivings are our own.
So in this psalm he rails against the blind

Injustice, as it seemed to him, when men
Who lived by exploitation did so well
At the expense of those they cheat. But then

You showed him truth beyond the daily veil
How wickedness will vanish like a dream
And when we wake in you all will be well.

Psalm 74: LXXIV *Ut quid, Deus?*

When we awake in you all will be well,
But now we feel your absence and we cry
'How long will the destroyers work their will?'

The random vandals who don't even try
To understand the good things they deface.
They trash the past, and cast a jaundiced eye

On all the works of beauty, art and grace
That once made up our culture. In their pride
They ruin things that no one can replace

As, making havoc of their lives, they slide
Back into chaos. Rouse us up, O Lord,
Who rode upon the seraphim. Divide

Once more the waters, draw the flaming sword,
Bring order out of chaos, as you did
When darkness fled before your holy Word.

Psalm 75: LXXV *Confitebimur tibi*

When darkness fled before your holy Word
You brought a world of beauty into being.
The sons of morning sang, creation heard

The song of heaven, and its echoes fleeing
Still stir a kind of music in our hearts,
As traces of that light transform our seeing.

And when we hear those echoes, heaven starts
A song in us that lifts us into praise.
You show us how the wickedness that hurts,

The sin that harms creation, the dark maze
Of our confusions, will be broken up
And cast aside. We lift our heads and gaze

At you in wonder, for we see the cup
The psalmist feared, so full of blood-red wine,
Is now a cup of blessing, life and hope.

Psalm 76: LXXVI *Notus in Judaea*

We lift the cup of blessing, life and hope
To one whose name has leapt from Israel
To circle all the world, who opens up

His heart to every nation. Weapons fail;
The sword and shield will rust; the tank and gun
Must come to nothing. Every dark betrayal

Of peace will come to judgement. For the one
Upon the throne will vindicate the meek
And turn our fierceness into praise: the Son

Of God, become the Son of Man. The weak
Will find their strength in him. He will restrain
The men of violence, but all who seek

Their peace in him will find it. And the stain
Of our blood-guiltiness will wash away
As heaven's mercy falls like gentle rain.

Psalm 77: LXVII *Voce mea ad Dominum*

As heaven's mercy falls like gentle rain,
I lift my face and let it wash me clean.
In all my times of trouble, darkness, pain,

I cry to him. I come to him and lean
Again into the comfort of his grace
And I remember all that he has been

To me in all my years of life. I trace
Once more the story of his steadfast love:
He sought me even when I turned my face

Away from him, descended from above
And found me in my hiding place. His might
Broke up my clouds of darkness, and he strove

Against the waves of chaos, in the night
Of my affliction, when he rescued me
And led me out of darkness into light.

Psalm 78: LXXVIII *Attendite, popule*

He led me out of darkness into light
And now I will proclaim all he has done
To rising generations. My delight

Will be to share the story of the one
Who came to me before I came to him,
Whose love still greets me with each rising sun.

But neither will I hide my sin and shame;
The many times that I refused his grace
And turned my back on him, forgot his name

And sought my former darkness, turned my face
Away from my redeemer. I'll confess
My own perversity, and dare to trace

My wilful trespass in the wilderness
And how through all of this, my Lord stayed true
And pulled me through with patient tenderness.

Psalm 79: LXXIX *Deus, venerunt*

He pulled me through with patient tenderness
And now I need his patience in my soul.
For now I feel the force of wickedness

And fear the worst in us will take control
And make a ruination of the best
As this long trial and crisis takes its toll.

The psalmist also faced this deadly test
So many dying every day, no space
Or even time to bury them. Pressed

On beyond what's possible, we face
Our dark dilemmas every day. We choose
For one another life or death. We race

Against the clock, and still we fear to lose
The lives we seek to save. O Jesus hear
Our sighs and pleas and bring us swift release.

Psalm 80: LXXX *Qui regis Israel*

Lord, hear our sighs and bring us swift release
For we have nothing left to us but tears,
No light, no joy, no strength, no health, no peace,

Only the strife, the dread, the strain, the fears
Of these dark times. Oh turn to us again,
Show us once more the mercy of those years

When you were forming us. Remember when
You called us out of exile, planted us
As your own vineyard. Was it all in vain

The way you tended us and nurtured us
That we might bear good fruit in joy and peace?
We have borne bitter fruit, but come to us

And help us start again. Come and release
With your right hand the grace we have refused,
Till shadows flee at last, and sorrows cease.

Psalm 81: LXXXI *Exultate Deo*

Till shadows flee at last, and sorrows cease
Come down and ease our shoulders from the burden
To give our straining hearts some soft release,

Lest from sheer weariness they shrink and harden.
Refresh us with the memory of grace,
Remind us of your mercy, of that pardon

You won for us forever from the cross.
Then we will lift a lighter song to you
And glimpse beyond our loneliness and loss

The lovely new moon shining, and the true
Signs of the kingdom coming, where they gleam
And kindle in the east, still showing through

This present darkness, even as a dream
Of light before the dawn. Send us a sign
That things are not so hopeless as they seem.

Psalm 82: LXXXII *Deus stetit*

For things are not so hopeless as they seem
God stands among the rulers as a judge.
He has no partiality. We deem

Ourselves better than others, hold a grudge
Against the stranger in our midst, reject
The ones who aren't like us, but he will judge

The world in righteousness. He will reject
The special pleading of the privileged.
And bless the meek instead. If we reflect

A little, in this earthly pilgrimage,
On how he loved the 'other' and the outcast
Then we will learn to share our heritage,

Not keep it only for our kin and caste,
But gather as the children of one King,
As kindred in our father's house at last.

Psalm 83: LXXXIII *Deus, quis similis?*

As kindred in our father's house at last
We will make peace with one another. Yet
We still make war; we still live in the past.

Even the psalmist here is filled with hate,
As gleefully he lists his enemies
And calls God's wrath upon them: 'let

Them perish, let them burn in flame' he cries,
And puts his curses in the mouth of God!
How can I pray this psalm? Give me the eyes

Of Jesus, help me see the iron rod
Which only crushes sin to free the sinful,
That I may know the holy name of God

Is not a name of wrath, but plentiful
Redemption. Name him: Jesus, *Yeshuah*
Yahweh saves, our God is merciful.

Psalm 84: LXXXIV *Quam dilecta!*

Yahweh saves, Our God is merciful
And how I long to enter in his courts
To nestle at his altar and to dwell

With him for ever. Day and night my thoughts
Are yearning towards the beauty of his temple
In swallow-flights of song. For in his courts

Time is transfigured, opened out and ample,
It touches on eternity. I stay
Awhile within this quiet church: its simple

Furnishings, and storied windows say
More to me of heaven than the pale
Abstractions of theology. A day

Spent in an empty church has been as full
Of goodness as an age elsewhere. I feel
Its peace refresh me like a holy well.

Psalm 85: LXXXV *Benedixisti, Domine*

His peace refreshes like a holy well,
His mercy turns me round and quickens me,
Lifts me a little higher for each fall.

And now within this psalm he summons me
To hear a truth my nation has ignored,
A truth forgotten in captivity.

So open me afresh to hear this word:
Mercy and truth are met together, peace
And righteousness have kissed each other. Lord,

How is it we have sundered them? Can peace
Be founded where there is no righteousness?
Some speak the truth, but speak it without grace

And, calling others out, are merciless.
Lord, join together all that we have sundered
That we may flourish in your tenderness.

Psalm 86: LXXXVI *Inclina, Domine*

That we may flourish in your tenderness
Bow down and hear the whispers of our fear
Our restless misery, our emptiness

Without you. Christ come close to me and hear!
Come close and comfort me in troubled times,
I need your mercy now for I despair

Of any other help. The telling chimes
Of every passing bell might be my own.
Lift up my soul, and breathe through my poor rhymes

That I might lay these lines before your throne
A frail *corona* wreathed of fading flowers
To set against the gold of David's crown,

Wrought in the pattern of my passing hours.
O you, who raised me from the depths of hell,
Kindle these lines with all your quickening powers.

Psalm 87: LXXXVII *Fundamenta ejus*

Kindle these lines with all your quickening powers,
For all my springs of life arise from you,
And like blind Milton in his midnight hours

I visit Sion's hill in dreams. I view
Siloam's sacred brook and bathe my soul
In those pure streams that cleanse me and renew

My vision and my purpose, make me whole
And sound again. The city of my God
Shines clear once more upon his holy hill,

My feet are set upon the royal road
That leads me through these shadowlands, until
I hear the trumpets, and set down my load

Beside the river bank and drink my fill
From that deep well of light at last and hear
My saviour's words of welcome: 'all is well!'

Psalm 88: LXXXVIII *Domine Deus*

My saviour's words of welcome: 'all is well'!
Was that just some false dream I used to have?
I tremble once more on the brink of hell,

Soon I'll be weeping in its lowest pit. The grave
Would be a kinder place than this. The dead
Forget, but I remember and I grieve

For all that I have lost: the green leaves shed
And stripped from me, my lovers and my friends
All torn away. Just emptiness and dread

Are my companions now. No one defends
Or speaks for me. Lord, I have cried to you
And you say nothing. Empty silence rends

My heart in pieces. There is no one who
Can find me now, for who could ever know
This agony unless they felt it too?

Psalm 89: LXXXIX *Misericordias Domini*

Who knows this agony unless they feel it too?
You answer me in darkness from your cross,
It is your pain that draws my heart to you

As deep calls unto deep and loss to loss.
Your covenant is sealed in your heart's blood
When it is pierced with mine. And our cries cross

In flesh and blood as I encounter God,
Not on the heights, but in the pit of hell.
Then I can sing the triumph of the good

Then I can truly know all will be well.
I recognise my saviour's mighty arm
Because it has been pierced. The bloody nail

Means more to me than those who see no harm
And keep God as a talisman, a spell
A cosy comforter, a lucky charm.

Psalm 90: XC *Domine, refugium*

A cosy comforter, a lucky charm?
Not with this psalmist, for he praises God
From everlasting ages, in his psalm.

A God of refuge – yes – and yet a God
Who knows the death that comes before each birth,
Who sees each generation die, a God

Before whom all the ages of the earth
Are like a passing day, like the cut grass
In Larkin's limpid verse: 'brief is the breath

Mown stalks exhale'. So we and all things pass,
And God endures beyond us. Yet he cares
For our brief lives, his loving tenderness

Extends to all his creatures, our swift years
Are precious in his sight. In Christ he shares
Our grief and he will wipe away our tears.

Psalm 91: XCI *Qui habitat*

He shares our grief and wipes away our tears
And even in this life he shelters us
Beneath the shadow of his wings. Our fears

And hopes are known to him. His faithfulness
Will be our shield and buckler. We can trust
His constancy and know he will be with us;

With us through the best and through the worst.
I may be threatened by the passing harm
Of outward pestilence, but still I trust

He gives his angels charge, and with his arm
He shelters and embraces me. No power
Can separate me from his love. His Name

Is my protection and delight. I pour
My heart and soul to him in songs and psalms,
And he will bring me through my darkest hour.

Psalm 92: XCII *Bonum est confiteri*

My Lord will bring me through my darkest hour,
And I will praise him in the morning light
And contemplate his wisdom and his power

Meeting together on the cross. By night
His truth will nurse and nurture me in dreams
And in the day my mind will still delight

In all his works and wisdom. The rich themes
Of his wise teaching shine through all I see:
The rushing winds and swiftly flowing streams

Will teach me of his spirit, the green tree
Will show his rooted fruitfulness, and I
Myself will flourish in his house and be

A tree that lifts its branches to the sky
Still bearing fruit for him in my old age
And trusting him until the day I die.

Psalm 93: XCIII *Dominus regnavit*

And trusting him until the day I die,
I will not fear the surging of the sea,
Though troubles in a floodtide rise so high;

Wave after wave of panic surges through me
And other people's fear and rage increase
My own, until the toxic mix is deadly.

But when it seems these troubles never cease
I sense beneath them all some solid ground,
A sure foundation and an inner peace,

And, overarching them, the starlit round
Of heaven's firmament. Though in between
The storms of life rage on, with all their sound

And fury, I still trust that all unseen,
Founded below and glorious above,
My saviour stands and keeps my soul serene.

Psalm 94: XCIV *Deus ultionum*

My saviour stands and keeps my soul serene
But also sends me back into the world
To speak his word and challenge the obscene

Injustices we take for granted, sold
As we are on systems that preserve
Our privilege and barter truth for gold,

Putting our souls to silence. We reserve
Our judgement, but the psalmist makes it clear
Justice is coming for God's poor. We serve

Him best if we can also serve them here,
Rise up and take their part against the proud
Deliver them from harassment and fear.

We have been pietistic, quiet, cowed
But we must come out publicly and cry
For equal rights and justice, cry out loud.

Psalm 95: XCV *Venite, exultemus*

For equal rights and justice, cry out loud!
Then come before God's presence and be glad,
And harden not your hearts. Do not be proud,

But kneel before your maker, for he made
You for himself and also for each other,
To share his good gifts equally. Our God

Is everyone's salvation, and our Father
Is Lord and father equally to all.
Let us rejoice before him, let him gather

The scattered tribes and nations back from all
The corners of the earth, and also from
The wilderness of willfulness. His call

To bring our lives, and our whole world to him
Resounds in all of us. Could we but hear,
Our Saviour, King and Shepherd calls us home.

Psalm 96: XCVI *Cantate Domino*

Our Saviour, King and Shepherd calls us home
And on our homeward journey bids us sing,
To join that all-renewing song to him

Which all creation sings. The valleys ring
With praises and the mountaintops rejoice;
The greenwood trees and meadow flowers bring

Their silent praise and call on us to voice
It for them in our songs, to worship him
In awe, in beauty, and in holiness.

It is not for ourselves alone we hymn
The great creator, for we lift our song
To voice creation's praise. The drowsy hum

Of honey-laden bees, the lovely, long
And lapsing sigh of waves along the shore,
And our own joy, must all make up the song.

Psalm 97: XCVII *Dominus regnavit*

With our own joy, we will take up the song
Of all creation: Jesus Christ is King!
The whole earth will be glad, for there has sprung

A light for all the righteous who will bring
A final judgement to the earth, as bright
As lightning, and the whole round world will ring

With jubilation. For the mournful night
Of our long exile will be ended then
As darkness flees before his glorious light,

The bright ark of his covenant. And when
We see that holiness unveiled, the dark
Devices, all the substitutes, the vain

And empty images, the shoddy work
Of our own hands will fall to nothingness
For Christ himself will shine as the true ark.

Psalm 98: XCVIII *Cantate Domino*

For Christ himself will shine as the true ark,
The holy one between the cherubim,
In his right hand and in his heart the mark

And imprint of the wounds we gave to him
Which he returns as love. He has declared
That love with open hands and heart. To him

The world with all its wounds, its shared
Desires and fears, will come, to seek the peace
Which he still offers freely. He has spared

The guilty, for he chose to take their place
And suffer for them. Therefore we will sing
A new song, in the all-renewing grace

Still flowing from those wounds. The world will ring
With music, drama, dance, and poetry,
With every gift that grateful hearts can bring.

Psalm 99: XCIX *Dominus regnavit*

With every gift that grateful hearts can bring
We celebrate the glory of the one
Who sits between the cherubim. We sing

A song of love and judgement met in one;
Mercy meets righteousness, and truth meets grace
Made one in Christ, as in him we are one.

The world may waver, we'll delight to trace
The long line of his loving, and to name
The holy ones who see him face to face:

Moses and Aaron, whom he has called home,
And Samuel. But I shall name each priest
Within my heritage, who looked to him:

John Donne and Herbert, Hopkins, each a priest
As much of language as of sacrament.
Love bids us welcome with them to the feast.

Psalm 100: C *Jubilate Deo*

Love bids us welcome with them to the feast
Let us be joyful therefore, let us sing
Old Hundredth with our forebears. One high priest

Calls us together in a great thanksgiving
To *come before his presence with a song,*
Enter his courts with praise, be glad and bring

Our very best to him. For we belong
To him since he has made us, and our hearts
Will find their peace in him alone. We long

Therefore to come at last beyond the gates
Of time and space, and with the saints to taste
That joy for which the whole creation waits.

But whilst we wait there is no time to waste
In keeping faith with each new generation,
And showing them his mercy and his grace.

Psalm 101: CI *Misericordiam et judicium*

I seek to show his mercy and his grace.
This psalmist sings of mercy and of judgement
Though reading on, there scarcely seems a trace

Of mercy in the way he casts that judgement
On everybody but himself: 'destroy
All the ungodly, give them punishment

And root them out'. He claims he won't employ
A servant whom he deems ungodly. Praise
Be to God that Christ has come, my joy

And my deliverance, whose steadfast gaze
Looks on me not with judgement but with grace.
My master is my servant, for his ways

Are not our ways. He kneels to make a place
For sinners at his table, welcomes all
Who turn, at any time, to seek his face.

Psalm 102: CII *Domine, exaudi*

I turn with my last gasp to seek your face
Before I turn my face back to the wall
And wither out my days, until my place

Is taken and my house deserted. All
My efforts come to nothing like the smoke
Of some stubbed cigarette whose thin blue veil

Drifts into emptiness, a bitter joke
That no one laughs at. Jesus are you there?
It seems a lonely lifetime since you spoke

Into my soul. O Jesus hear my prayer
Turn back to me or turn me back to you,
For I am on the brink of black despair.

But you are sure and steadfast, only you
Can save me now. Rekindle my desire
And draw me out of death and into you.

Psalm 103: CIII *Benedic, anima mea*

You drew me out of death and into you,
You saved my life and crowned me with your love.
I played you false but you stayed strong and true.

I sank below, but you reached from above
And set me on a firm foundation, showed
Once more the way of mercy, truth and love.

You lifted from my shoulders the dark load
Of all my sin and flung it far from me
As far as east from west. Now all my road

Lies open, and with eager eyes I see
The places you prepare for me to go,
The tasks that you appoint and set for me.

I know my weakness but I also know
Your strength will be at work in me. For you
Cast down the mighty and exalt the low.

Psalm 104: CIV *Benedic, anima mea*

Cast down the mighty and exalt the low,
My God upon whose breath all life is borne,
As on the wind's swift wings, when, sweeping low

You lift the mists and drive the clouds, all drawn
Aloft by flaming ministers. The light
Throughout the cosmos is your veil, withdrawn

To show your glory once, for you were light
Itself made flesh in that transfiguration.
You make the day, and in the tender night

The moon and stars shine as a revelation
Of your transcendent beauty, for you shine
In all your works, and breathe through all creation.

In every woven strand of life the line
Of your strong love is drawn and gathered in,
Knotted and crowned in Christ and made divine.

Psalm 105: CV *Confitemini Domino*

Knotted and crowned in Christ and made divine:
As with creation, so with history.
Through Israel's ancient tales we trace Christ's line

From Abraham to Isaac, till we see
In Joseph, Jacob's son, the one whose sum
Of life becomes itself a prophecy,

A pattern of compassion yet to come:
For he became a slave, was bought and sold,
Yet all his suffering was foreseen, his shame

Became his glory as his dreams foretold.
And likewise Moses shadows these things forth
In stories of salvation that unfold

For us the depth and meaning of our faith.
Christ shimmers through these scriptures when our minds
Are cleansed and kindled by his spirit's breath.

Psalm 106: CVI *Confitemini Domino*

I'm cleansed and kindled by his spirit's breath,
But I'm no sooner cleansed than I defile
Myself again, and turn from life to death,

My kindlings all as cold as ash. This tale
Of Israel's backslidings speaks to me,
For I too was delivered and like Israel

Strayed in the wilderness. I turn and see
The shards of all my golden calves, my old
Attempts to turn the holy mystery

Into a thing of my own making, gold
And glittering, but lifeless in the end.
Yet I take comfort from this psalm. The old

Tales help me as I see my God extend
His patience and still keep his covenant;
My judge is still my saviour and my friend.

Psalm 107: CVII *Confitemini Domino*

My judge is still my saviour and my friend.
Time after time he finds and rescues me,
Makes a beginning where I've made an end.

I was astray and yet he came to me
And filled my hungry soul with nourishment.
I sat in darkness, bound in misery,

Crushed by depression and discouragement,
He brought me out of darkness, broke the chain,
The complex links of my imprisonment.

When I was sick and wearied and in pain,
Afraid of pestilence in these dark days,
He sent his Word and raised me up again.

So I will sing this psalm that sings his praise,
Telling of all the wonders he has done,
Whose loving-kindness keeps me all my days.

Psalm 108: CVIII *Paratum cor meum*

Your loving-kindness keeps me all my days
And I awake already found in you,
An instrument you tune to sing your praise.

If I could only listen, and stay true
To what my heart's already singing, hear
The deeper music that it sounds in you,

Turn down the white noise of my busyness,
And in that waiting silence could awake
To my heart's song, in that rich openness

To hear your heartbeat in my own, and take
My living rhythm from your heart in mine.
Then I might live and love, not for my sake

But yours. Then everywhere I might divine
The music of your mercy, as I draw
The water of my life and find it wine.

Psalm 109: CIX *Deus laudem*

The water of my life may turn to wine,
This psalmist turns it into vinegar,
Such is his bitterness, and his design

To wish the worst upon his foe, to bear
Down on him with vengeance and to see
His children suffer too. No pity here,

Only the anger of an injury
Unhealed, and an injustice unforgiven.
'My heart', he cries, 'is wounded deep within me

I go hence like a shadow, I am driven
Away'. And so he cries aloud 'Oh save me'!
And my heart too is wounded, broken, riven

I also ask, O Lord, that you should save me:
Save me from bitterness and heal my heart
That even for my foes I might ask mercy.

Psalm 110: CX *Dixit Dominus*

That even for my foes I might ask mercy,
I come to one who is both judge and priest,
And sits at God's right hand. My enemy

Is just as close to him as I, the least
Amongst us loved as dearly as the best.
From furthest west out to the utter east

He gathers us for judgement, but the test
Is not what we've achieved but whom we have
Forgiv'n. The Judge condemns the sin, but lest

We should despair, the Priest comes down to save
The sinner. Like Melchisedech, he bears
Both bread and wine for us. For these he gave

His life in sacrifice and now he shares
Our suffering. He is the wounded King
Whose holy wounds are always healing ours.

Psalm 111: CXI *Confitebor tibi*

His holy wounds are always healing ours,
I will give thanks to him with my whole heart,
When I'm alone in all those secret hours

Of intimate encounter, set apart,
And also in the congregation, where
Our voices join and 'heart speaks unto heart'.

And I will marvel at his works, and stare
Delighted at a dewdrop, or the beauty
In tiny grains of sand, for everywhere

I see his laws at work; his verity
And judgement underlie each separate thing
That he has made. In each the mystery

From which all things arise still seems to sing.
I hear it and begin, with holy fear
And awe, to trace his Word in everything.

Psalm 112: CXII *Beatus vir*

With awe I trace his Word in everything
And ask his blessing on me. I delight
To know his wisdom and his mercy, sing

Aloud of all his judgements. There's a light
That shines in darkness, and the brooding dark
Will never put it out or comprehend it.

And now I pray that Christ himself will work
In me, that through my words and deeds he'll bless
The world he loves, that I will never shirk

The call to lend a little of his grace
To all who need it, that I will not shrink
From sharing all I have, that I'll redress

As best I can the world's injustice, drink
So deeply from the well of life that I
May bring all those who thirst back to its brink.

Psalm 113: CXIII *Laudate, pueri*

I bring my thirsty soul back to the brink
Of that deep well, the fount of life and light
From which the poor and rich alike must drink.

I make his name my praise and my delight,
For he has lifted me out of the mire
And raised me from the dust, set me upright

From every fall, and every false desire.
From every sunrise until every dusk
His patient love has guided me. The fire

Of his consuming love has burnt the husk
And chaff that cloaks and chokes his holy seed
Until the grain shines clear. And now my task

Is set: to till the ground, uproot the weed,
Prepare the dark soil of my growing soul
That I might bear the fruit of his good seed.

Psalm 114: CXIV *In exitu Israel*

That I might bear the fruit of his good seed
I hear again the tale of his redemption:
The one true Exodus, the mighty deed

That set his people free, the liberation
Not just of Israel out of Egypt's bond
But of all people out of condemnation,

Out of the slavery of sin. His hand
Has overthrown the devil's tyranny
And now he leads us to our promised land.

For Christ, like Moses, comes to part the sea,
The dark red sea of death, and by his blood
He has redeemed us. All humanity

Was gathered in him on the cross, the flood
That might have drowned us has been driven back,
He brought us through forever and for good.

Psalm 115: CXV *Non nobis, Domine*

He brought us through forever and for good,
Not unto us, but to his name be praise!
And still they ask me, where is now your God?

As though the giver of all nights and days,
The maker of the stars, whose love sustains
The smallest atom and the brilliant blaze

Of galaxies, as though the God who reigns
Was one more item in the list of things
We catalogue and think we can explain,

One of our idols, one of those small things
Our minds construct and end up worshipping!
He is in heaven. Yet he gives us wings

To rise to him, and gives us words to sing,
If we'll forsake our vain imaginings
And recognise our risen Lord and King.

Psalm 116: CXVI *Dilexi, quoniam*

I recognise our risen Lord and King
And turn again to find my rest in him,
For I have been in trouble. I will bring

The anguish of my soul once more to him
Who feels that anguish with me. Misery
And all the snares of death made faith so dim,

My prayer was just a whisper. But he heard me,
He raised my head and called me to look up,
And now he asks one simple thing of me:

To let him love me, to take up the cup
Of my salvation and to make a new
Communion in his love. He is the hope

Of all the earth and soon he will renew
His whole creation in the risen Son
Whose love is steadfast and whose word is true.

Psalm 117: CXVII *Laudate Dominum*

His Love is steadfast and his Word is true
His mercy and his kindness will endure
For evermore. I praise my saviour who

Descended and became one of the poor,
Came down with us to death that he might raise
Us up. 'His kindness is for evermore'

The psalmist says, who wrote this in the days
Before the resurrection. I will make
This little psalm the springboard of my praise

Who have more cause to praise him. I will take
These words and find The Word himself in them;
The promise of the day when we awake

From darkness into light, and look on him
Who found us deep in death and drew us out
That we might shine amidst the seraphim.

Psalm 118: CXVIII *Confitemini Domino*

That we might shine amidst the seraphim
He made himself much lower than the angels
And dwelt with us that we might dwell with him.

He did not stay amongst the cloudy symbols
Of abstract speculation but became
The cosmic cornerstone. And so all angles

Of our approach to God must meet in him.
And yet he was the stone that we rejected,
Though every builder must be built in him,

His one true light in every life refracted.
This is his doing – it is marvelous!
In each of us his image is reflected

Like light upon a stream. I trace its course
Upstream towards the fountain whence it flows
And end in my beginning and my source.

Psalm 119: CXIX *Beati immaculati*

I end in my beginning and my source,
The one who is my life, my truth, my way.
*A*nd *b*lessed are the ones who in the *c*ourse

Of life *de*sire to *f*ind and keep that way,
Who *g*ive themselves to studying *hi*s Word.
*J*oy shall lead them, *k*now*l*edge *m*ake their way

So plai*n* bef*o*re their eyes. The *p*erfect Lord
Comes down to *q*uicken us, *rest*ore our so*u*l,
Remove the *v*eil *w*e place over his Word,

And fi*x* our eyes on merc*y*, as the whole
And only meaning of the Law. To prove
And to fulfil that truth, his heart and soul

Were poured out when he came down from above,
That all the letters in the Law of *Z*ion
Might now become the alphabet of Love.

The italic letters, from A to Z, reflect that each of the sections of the original psalm is headed by a different letter of the Hebrew alphabet in alphabetical sequence.

Psalm 120: CXX *Ad Dominum*

These letters are an alphabet of love,
And every word I spell speaks of his grace.
And now I need that grace! I need to prove

The power of the things that make for peace,
For I am set amidst the enemies
Of peace, the warriors who soon release

Their flaming arrows and who never cease
To stir up trouble and to kindle flame
With falsehoods, with incendiary lies.

O hear me when I call upon your name
Keep me in patience; keep me in your peace.
When I'm attacked let me not give the same

As I receive or seek redress. Release
Me from the cycle of revenge and bring
My soul into the haven of your peace.

Psalm 121: CXXI *Levavi oculos*

Oh how I seek the haven of your peace,
For though I lift my eyes up to the hills
There is no help from them and no release

From all my restless troubles, all the ills
That still oppress my soul. My help will come
From God alone, whose loving presence fills

And overflows my heart. The restless drum
Of my anxieties is stilled. He'll keep
My soul in perfect peace, summon and sum

The best in me to blossom, and still weep
With me for all that I have lost. He'll hold
Me close to him whether I wake or sleep

Shade me by day or night, always enfold
Me in his love. His alchemy of grace
Transmutes my leaden life into pure gold.

Psalm 122: CXXII *Laetatus sum*

Transmute my leaden life into pure gold
And draw me home to your Jerusalem
Along that golden string that I still hold

Since Blake first put it in my hand. The hem
Of Jesus' garment was enough to start
The healing. After that, I followed him

And found the holy city of the heart:
The true Jerusalem, city of peace.
The peace we ask of God can only start

Within his people. Wars will only cease
When we refuse to fight. Instead we'll pray,
We'll draw the bow of burning gold, release

The arrows of desire that wing their way
And quiver in the kingdom, draw us all
Beyond the gates of everlasting day.

Psalm 123: CXXIII *Ad te levavi oculos meos*

Beyond the gates of everlasting day,
Up to the starry threshold of the heavens
I lift my eyes. I lift my eyes and pray:

I pray to be remembered, and forgiven.
I look for you in longing and I wait
Upon you as your servant. You have given

Day-labour for your servant to complete,
But nothing can be done without your grace
Without your kindling spirit, so I wait

Upon your mercy, till you turn your face
And bless my work. Then, let the world despise,
And the sophisticated sneer, in my place

However small, I have a role I prize
As one scribe of the kingdom. I rejoice
And, with this psalmist, lift my grateful eyes.

Psalm 124: CXXIV *Nisi quia Dominus*

With every psalm I lift my grateful eyes,
For if you had not come to comfort me
This task would overwhelm me. The sheer size

Of such an undertaking daunted me,
My doubts and my misgivings would have stayed
My hand. I praise you now, who set me free

From every snare, and from the fears that preyed
Upon my mind, encouraged me to fly
Into the heights for you. The sins that weighed

Me down are dealt with, set aside, and I
Can rise upon your wings again and sing,
Glad as the lark that carols in the sky.

I meditate your psalms at night and bring
These fruits to you each morning, offering
This linked *corona* to my Lord and King.

Psalm 125: CXXV *Qui confidunt*

This linked *corona* for my Lord and King,
This daily-woven wreathe of little flowers
I lay before you as an offering

In thankfulness for mercy. All my powers
Of expression, my delight in words
Are gifts that come from you. The idle hours

That give me time to find and weave these words
All flow to me from you, and all my trust
Is in your steadfast love. The singing birds

That flit from branch to branch, and make their nest
Safe in the cedars, these all look to you
As I do, and, with me, you give them rest.

We flitter on the winds of time, but you
Stand steadfast as the hills. Because you rise
Beyond all change, we find our peace in you.

Psalm 126: CXXVI *In convertendo*

Beyond all change, we find our peace in you,
And you turn our captivity to joy
And fill our mouths with laughter, for in you

We find that we ourselves are found. The joy
You give, no one can take from us. We sow
In tears it's true, but nothing can destroy

The promise hidden in the seeds we sow:
The promise of our coming resurrection.
For death has been defeated, and we know

That when death comes for us, breathing destruction,
The life he comes to take is safely hidden
With Christ in God, awaiting resurrection.

The first fruit of that harvest once lay hidden
And sealed in secret in a garden tomb
But we will rise in him, for he is risen!

Psalm 127: CXXVII *Nisi Dominus*

Since we will rise in him, for he is risen,
We also seek to live and work in him.
For only what is done in him, and given

Back to him, can live. And all the grim
Exactions of the greedy world will fall
To nothing on that day. For without him

Our labour is in vain. In vain we call
On others for their overtime, and in vain
'Increase our productivity' for all

The works of this wide world: the loss and gain,
'Getting and spending', pressing others on
To more consumption, all the stress and pain

That we inflict on others, exploitation
Of weary workers and a weary world,
Must come to judgement, death, and resurrection.

Psalm 128: CXXVIII *Beati omnes*

We come to judgement, death, and resurrection
Sooner or later. We must seek his ways,
Not for 'success', but for a true fruition.

I'm thankful that the labour of my days
Has borne sufficient fruit that I may put
Bread on the table, but far more I praise

Him for this lasting gift, the grace, the fruit
Of family, the strong companionship
Of wife and children, praise him for the root

And ground of love, the heartfelt fellowship
Of a long marriage. For I might have been
Alone in life, bereft of love and friendship,

But I've been blessed with both, and I have seen
My children flourish, and the fruitful vine
We planted years ago still young and green.

Psalm 129: CXXIX *Saepe expugnaverunt*

The vine we planted is still young and green,
For all the old assaults of wind and weather.
Likewise I know that I myself have seen

Some bitter times when things conspired together
To break me, when they nearly ploughed me under.
I understand this psalmist, and I'd rather

Complain to God than not, but still I wonder
If he was right to call on God to smite
His enemies. As though that holy thunder

Were just a private weapon, and the fight
Were always just, and God was on our side
And we were always only in the right.

Better to ask for mercy, mercy wide
As the wide ocean. If my enemy
And I *both* ask, we will not be denied.

Psalm 130: CXXX *De profundis*

Ask him for mercy, you won't be denied.
Call on him *de profundis*, from the deep;
The places where the child in you has cried

All night unheard, and where your spirit weeps
As Rachael wept and would not be consoled.
Cry from the place where grief unspoken seeps

Into a bitter silence, never told
And never healed. So cry out from the deep:
Bring every grief to God, do not withhold

A tear from him. Give him your tears to keep
For they are precious to him. Flee to him,
His heart was pierced and he knows how to weep,

For he is full of mercy, and with him
Is plenteous redemption. Let him sound
The depths that he might draw you out from them.

Psalm 131: CXXXI *Domine, non est*

You sound the depths to draw me out from them.
And though I feel the trauma of what's past,
I simply cling to you and feel no shame

In my complete dependence. For at last
I've found the one who fully cares for me,
The one in whom I can completely trust.

And yet in that dependence I am free,
Weaned from a false reliance on the world
With its click-baited co-dependency.

Instead I lean on you, and I am held
So gently, and I nestle in so near,
That pride and haughtiness just lose their hold,

Worldliness falls away from me. I hear
Your heartbeat and I feel the pulse of love,
The perfect love that casts out every fear.

Psalm 132: CXXXII *Memento, Domine*

The perfect love that casts out every fear,
Came down with the Christ, the true anointed one,
Whose coming David saw when *Yahweh* swore

One of his line, Messiah, David's son
Would sit upon his throne and wear his crown.
But David died before the deed was done,

Nor did he ever know the promised crown
Would be a crown of thorns, the 'resting place'
Would be the sepulchre. God would come down

And earth would meet with heaven face to face,
And when Christ 'satisfied the poor with bread'
That bread would be his body. In our place

He would face death and suffer in our stead
To set us right. And now the crown of thorns
Is bright with blossom round his sacred head.

Psalm 133: CXXXIII *Ecce, quam bonum!*

The crown still blossoms round his sacred head
And he would also wreathe us altogether
Gathered in him. Though we have all been led

By many different paths, at last we gather
And find that all our paths have led to him,
Whether his beauty drew us here, or whether

It was companionship in grief. The hem
Of his good garment spreads that everyone
May touch it at some moment, as for them

His power of healing flows. And then the Son
Calls them to turn and meet him face to face,
Feel after him and find him, and to join

With all the others who have felt his grace.
It is indeed a good and joyful thing
To gather in one love and in one place.

Psalm 134: CXXXIV *Ecce nunc*

To gather in one love and in one place,
To lift our hands up in the sanctuary,
Singing by candlelight and face to face,

Bathing our souls in love's own liturgy,
Praising the God who made both earth and heaven,
Sensing his presence and his mystery,

To give him thanks for all that we are given,
Is both a joy and blessing. Evening falls;
We end the day redeemed, fulfilled, forgiven,

Ready to rest in him; and, when he calls,
To rise with him and greet the day with praise,
That all this hallowed ground, the courts and halls

Which echoed with our evening prayer, may raise
A new song in the morning, that his name
May bless our nights and sanctify our days.

Psalm 135: CXXXV *Laudate Nomen*

To bless our nights and sanctify our days
We praise and magnify his holy Name:
The Name behind all names, the Name whose praise

Is ringing through creation. For he came
Into his cosmos, and he formed and chose
A people for himself. And when the days

Had been fulfilled, was born and died and rose,
That he might rescue and redeem us all.
These are his mighty deeds. The psalmist chose

Those stories from *his* past that might recall
God's mighty power at work in history,
But all those tribal victories, and all

The songs that celebrate their memory
Can only shadow forth, anticipate,
What came in Christ: the cosmic victory!

Psalm 136: CXXXVI *Confitemini*

What came in Christ, the cosmic victory
Was given in his everlasting mercy.
The angel's message and the grace of Mary

Were given in his everlasting mercy.
His holy childhood and obedience
Were given in his everlasting mercy.

His three temptations and his strong resistance
Were given in his everlasting mercy.
His gifts of bread and wine in such abundance

Were given in his everlasting mercy.
His teaching and his call to true repentance
Were given in his everlasting mercy.

His bitter passion and his great endurance
Were given in his everlasting mercy.
That we might find in Christ complete assurance.

Psalm 137: CXXXVII *Super flumina*

That we might find in Christ complete assurance
We still recall these stories of the past,
For in them is the pattern and persistence

Of our long exile from the things that last.
For we live *super flumina*: time flows
Away from us, and all we prize is lost

The moment we attain it, like the rose
That shows eternity yet fades and falls.
So all our songs and music still disclose

The tragedy of time. The voice that calls
Us from eternity must always make
An elegy. We beat against time's walls,

For this is Babylon. Our captors take
The best in us the moment it is born.
But Babylon will fall! We will awake!

Psalm 138: CXXXVIII *Confitebor tibi*

Great Babylon will fall! We will awake!
'One short sleep past, we wake eternally'
And even now the poets rise and shake

Us up a little, waken us to see
'The loveliness and wonder', turn our eyes
Towards your temple and the mystery

Which lives within us, and will also rise
And dawn upon the world. The poets sing.
They sing, and in their singing make us wise.

Though I am in the midst of troubles, bring
Me through them with your mighty hand, restore
Me and refresh my soul, that I may sing

With all the poets: those who came before
And stand before you now, and those you call
This very night to worship and adore.

Psalm 139: CXXXIX *Domine, probasti*

This very night I worship and adore
For I am drawn towards your mystery.
I cannot fully know you, but before

I was conceived you knew and summoned me.
You called me into being. I was formed
Both in my mother's womb and in the sea

Of your strong love. The blood that warmed
My growing body also flowed in you,
When you were hid in Mary's womb and formed

In our humanity. I turn to you
Because you know my heart better than I,
The darkness there was never dark to you.

However low I fall, however high
I rise, your loving presence meets me there
And you will still be with me when I die.

Psalm 140: CXL *Eripe me, Domine*

I know you will be with me when I die,
Yet even in this life deliver me.
For there is malice in the world and I

Am fearful of the wickedness I see,
Especially the malice of the tongue:
The spreading lies, the slander, and the glee

With which a call-out culture seems to hang
Such defamation on the ones who differ,
Or change the party line, how they harangue

And bully, and how much their victims suffer.
I understand the psalmist's anger here:
'A man who's full of words shall never prosper'

And so I read with trembling and with fear.
Lord, sift my words, and make them generous,
Make them capacious, open, lucid, clear.

Psalm 141: CXLI *Domine, clamavi*

Make me capacious, open, lucid, clear.
Consider well my voice, Lord, when I cry,
Then guard and guide my lips lest you should hear

From me the new-speak of my time: the sly
Evasion of the facts, the subtle sneer
Equivocating truth into a lie.

But open up my lips that you might hear
The song you gave me at my birth: a song
Of love and yearning, strong enough to bear

Our burdens up with beauty, through this long
And aching exile, a lament,
A song to gather scattered bones, a song

To bring down Babylon, whose violent
Oppression tries to drown us out, a song
That turns all sorrow into sacrament.

Psalm 142: CXLII *Voce mea ad Dominum*

You turn my sorrow into sacrament.
I cry to you and pour out my complaint
And you transmute my bitterness. You sent

Your spirit like a leaven, took the taint
Of my resentment in your alchemy
And turned the lead to gold. In the 'blent

Air' of every church, the litany
Of suffering that rises up in prayer
Is changed to glory. Through the mystery

Of your atonement, you take our despair,
If we will only offer it to you,
And turn it into hope. Because you share

In all our suffering, we know that you
Will bring us with you through that suffering
To share your glory, as we worship you.

Psalm 143: CXLIII *Domine, exaudi*

We share your glory as we worship you
And so I ask, each morning, 'hear my prayer'.
I bring my desolation back to you,

I do not hide from you the deep despair
That still afflicts me sometimes. I recall
The many times you've helped me, all the care

And love you've shown, your patience when I fall,
How every time you've lifted me again
And called me back to you. I think of all

The times when darkness fell, and in my pain
I cried aloud and lifted up my hands
To you from thirsty lands. Time and again

Your loving spirit led me forth, my bonds
Were broken, and I took the pilgrim path
Towards your Easter, out of Lenten lands.

Psalm 144: CXLIV *Benedictus Dominus*

Towards your Easter, out of Lenten lands
I walk each day upon my pilgrimage,
And every day you guide me, teach my hands

Their art and their resistance: to engage
In warfare, not against poor flesh and blood,
But to resist the powers of this age

In spiritual warfare, setting good
Against each evil, where the battle line
Runs right through every heart. O Lord, you stood

For all humanity, you held the line
Against the devil when you overthrew
The hosts of evil there on Calvary.

Bow down the heavens, come down and renew
In me your victory, reclaim my heart
And turn my inmost being back to you.

Psalm 145: CXLV *Exaltabo te, Deus*

I turn my inmost being back to you
To magnify and praise you from my heart,
Whose heart is loving and whose word is true,

Delighting in this psalm, which played a part
In my conversion, forty years ago.
An unbeliever then, I thought I'd start

To read the Bible as a poet, so
I started with the psalms. And I recall
The single verse that changed me and would show

Me hope at last: *The Lord upholdest all,*
All such as fall, also *he lifteth up*
All those that are down ... the eyes of all

Wait upon thee. And then a sudden hope
Sprang up in me, that somewhere in that *all*
I might be found. I knelt down, and looked up!

Psalm 146: CXLVI *Lauda, anima mea*

I have been found! I kneel down and look up
With all the fallen whom your hand upholds.
Morning by morning you renew my hope,

That as you draw me from the gentle folds
Of sleep, you'll draw me from the snares of death.
I'll live to praise the one whose love upholds

The universe from end to end. Each breath
Is praise and when at last my soul goes forth
On my last breath, you'll bring me up from death

And into life with you. As on this earth
You loose us from our prisons and defend
The stranger and the fatherless, in dearth

You feed the hungry, and in darkness send
Your light to heal our blindness, even so
We'll know you as our King, world without end.

Psalm 147: CXLVII *Laudate Dominum*

We'll know you as our King, world without end
And praise you in the heavens, when you gather
The outcasts in, and all your children stand

Before you in true Sion, held together
In your love, all heartbreak healed at last.
Till then we'll praise the goodness of our Father,

Our Saviour and the Spirit, who has blessed
And breathes through all creation. Every star
Is known to him and named, from first to last.

He gives his snow like wool, and near and far
The sharp frost and the flowing streams in spring,
Each growing seed and blade of grass, the sheer

Abundance and the plenitude of things,
The whirling atoms, all live in his Word
And wait to hear the whole creation sing.

Psalm 148: CXLVIII *Laudate Dominum*

We wait to hear the whole creation sing,
But even here, redeemed, we start the song,
Begin the praise of heaven's Lord and King.

So praise him all you angels, all the throng
Of beings whose intelligence and love
Our mortal minds can scarcely grasp, and whose

Energy and joy reaches above
Our range, yet sometimes glimmers through the veil
Of our own Eucharist. Our partial love

Is joined with theirs in singing *Holy, Holy*
Holy is the Lord, the earth and heaven
Are full of glory. One day we'll be wholly

Drawn up into that *sanctus*, we'll be given
A harmony with all created things,
As earth herself is lifted into heaven.

Psalm 149: CXLIX *Cantate Domino*

When earth herself is lifted into heaven
The song we sing will be forever new,
And even now, the ransomed and forgiven

Live out that newness in their hearts, renew
The world around them with their praise. We dance
To tunes the world has never heard, for you

Put heaven's music in our hearts. The stance
Of praise is radical: a two-edged sword!
We cut through all the cords of change and chance

For we keep heaven's time. The living Word
Is on our lips, and the usurping power
Of this dark age must tremble, for he's heard

The proclamation of his doom. The hour
Of our deliverance has come. For we
Are buried seeds whose time has come to flower.

Psalm 150: CL *Laudate Dominum*

For buried seeds the time has come to flower,
To blossom into victory and praise.
So praise God in his firmament of power

Whose only power is love: the power to raise
The dead to life, the power to restore
The lost, and turn our long lament to praise.

Oh praise him in his noble acts and for
His great redemption. Praise him with the sound
Of trumpets. Tune your music at the door

He is about to open. Beat the ground
With light and loosened feet, for all his ways
Are glory, and all places hallowed ground.

So come and bring him all your nights and days,
And come into his courts with joyful song,
Come to the place where every breath is praise.